MAKING THE MIRACLE

THE BIGGEST COMEBACKS IN SPORTS

by Eric Braun

CAPSTONE PRESS
a capstone imprint

Published by Capstone Press, an imprint of Capstone
1710 Roe Crest Drive, North Mankato, Minnesota 56003
capstonepub.com

SPORTS ILLUSTRATED KIDS is a trademark of ABG-SI LLC.
Used with permission.

Library of Congress Cataloging-in-Publication Data
Names: Braun, Eric, 1971- author.
Title: Making the miracle : the biggest comebacks in sports / by Eric Braun.
Description: North Mankato, Minnesota : Capstone Press, [2023] | Series: Sports illustrated kids. Heroes and heartbreakers | Includes bibliographical references and index. | Audience: Ages 8-11 | Audience: Grades 4-6 | Summary: "Second-half reversals, amazing wins after long-standing droughts, and more! In this Sports Illustrated Kids book, discover the all-time biggest comebacks in sports history. Read about Michael Jordan's miraculous return after retirement. Discover more about the largest comeback in Super Bowl history. And don't forget Bethany Hamilton's unmatched return to surfing after a shark attack! With eye-popping photographs and heart-pounding text, this book will be a surefire hit with sports fans, young and old"— Provided by publisher.
Identifiers: LCCN 2022029360 (print) | LCCN 2022029361 (ebook) | ISBN 9781669011156 (hardcover) | ISBN 9781669011101 (paperback) | ISBN 9781669011118 (pdf) | ISBN 9781669011132 (kindle edition)
Subjects: LCSH: Comebacks—History—Juvenile literature. | Sports—History—Juvenile literature.
Classification: LCC GV705.4 .B736 2023 (print) | LCC GV705.4 (ebook) | DDC 796—dc23/eng/20220721
LC record available at https://lccn.loc.gov/2022029360
LC ebook record available at https://lccn.loc.gov/2022029361

Editorial Credits
Editor: Carrie Sheely; Designer: Elyse White; Media Researcher: Morgan Walters; Production Specialist: Whitney Schaefer

Image and Design Element Credits
Associated Press: 13, Eric Risberg, 9, Scott Strazzante, 9; Getty Images: JOHN GURZINSKI/AFP, 29, Brian Lawdermilk, 22, 23, Claus Bergmann/Conti Press, 20, David E. Klutho, 14, Icon Sport, 11, Sean Rowland, 19, TASOS KATOPODIS/AFP, 15; Library of Congress: Prints & Photographs Division, 16; Newscom: Sport the Library, 18; Shutterstock: afaf.asf design element (surfer icon), aPhoenix photographer, cover (background) , Gorodenkoff, 5, IYIKON, design element (boxing icon), Jacob Lund, 4, kuroksta, design element (soccer icon), NDAB Creativity, cover (bottom), Palsur, design element (icons), Pavel Kukol, design element (racing icon); Sports Illustrated: Chuck Solomon, 17, Manny Millan, 21, 25, 26, 27, Robert Beck, 7

Source Notes
Page 8, "This is what . . . " Jason Lloyd, "The Comeback, No. 3: LeBron brings joy to a city used to painful losses," The Athletic, September 7, 2020, https://theathletic.com/2009580/2020/09/07/the-comeback-no-3-lebron-brings-joy-to-a-city-used-to-painful-losses/
Page 11, "You could tell . . . " Simon Hughes and James Pearce, "The Comeback, No. 6: Liverpool pull off football's greatest miracle in Istanbul," September 2, 2020, https://theathletic.com/2040184/2020/09/03/the-comeback-no-6-liverpool-pull-of-footballs-greatest-miracle-in-istanbul/
Page 12, "You are going to . . . " Manny Randhawa, "Steve Bartman and the 15 Biggest All-Time Villains of the Chicago Cubs," October 25, 2011, https://bleacherreport.com/articles/909708-steve-bartman-and-the-15-biggest-all-time-villains-of-the-chicago-cubs
Page 24, "I'm back." J.A. Adande, "Michael Jordan's famous 'I'm back' fax, 25 years later," March 18, 2020, https://www.espn.com/nba/story/_/id/12501628/michael-jordan-famous-back-fax-25-years-later
Page 28, "For 10 years, . . . " Jenny Dial Creech, "The Comeback, No. 28: George Foreman's return to the ring, in his own words," August 12, 2020, https://theathletic.com/1980133/2020/08/12/the-comeback-no-28-george-foremans-return-to-the-ring-in-his-own-words/
Websites accessed March 2022.

All internet sites appearing in back matter were available and accurate when this book was sent to press.

TABLE OF CONTENTS

Words in **bold** are in the glossary.

THE THRILL OF A COMEBACK

A lot of sports fans might prefer an easy victory. It's nice when you can relax knowing that the win is in the bag. Many athletes might feel the same way. It's easier to coast to the finish line than to fight for a win.

But let's be honest. There's nothing more fun than a comeback. Comebacks are those moments when great players shine. Those are the "I can't believe it!" moments. The "How did they do that?" moments. The bite-your-fingernails, pace-the-floor, shout-at-the-TV moments.

Some comebacks happen in the biggest games. Some are the story of one person battling long odds. However they happen, comebacks take incredible skill and grit. Comebacks are sports at their best.

CHAPTER 1
CHAMPIONSHIP COMEBACKS

Athletes play for the glory of winning it all. They don't want to watch the championship on TV. They want to be holding the trophy. For fans, there's no greater joy than watching their favorite team compete for the biggest prize. And if they can see a thrilling comeback win—even better!

SUPER BOWL LI

By the fourth quarter of Super Bowl LI on February 5, 2017, the Atlanta Falcons led the New England Patriots 28–9. But New England kicked a field goal. Then they sacked Falcons quarterback Matt Ryan and forced a fumble. They turned that into a quick touchdown, and added a 2-point conversion. The comeback was on. The Patriots tied the game by scoring 19 points in less than 10 minutes!

The game went into overtime. But by then New England had all the **momentum**. They won the coin toss and marched down the field for the game-winning touchdown.

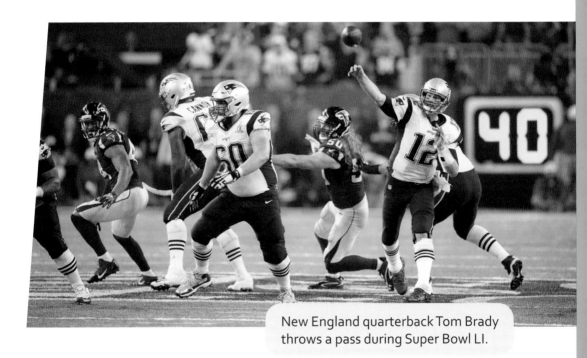

New England quarterback Tom Brady throws a pass during Super Bowl LI.

FUN FACT

In NFL postseason history, no team had blown a fourth-quarter lead as big as the Falcons had in Super Bowl LI.

BRINGING IT HOME

LeBron James started his pro career playing for his hometown team, the Cleveland Cavaliers. In 2010, he went to Miami, but he returned to Cleveland in 2014. He badly wanted to bring a championship to his hometown. Cleveland hadn't won a title in any pro sport in 52 years. Two years later, the Cavaliers made it to the 2016 NBA championship. They took on the powerful Golden State Warriors. But when the Cavaliers got down three games to one, the chances did not look good.

The Cavaliers came through to win Games 5 and 6. So Game 7 was on back in Oakland, California. Late in the fourth quarter, the game was tied at 89. That's when James made a stunning block on a layup attempt. It set the tone for a big finish. Kyrie Irving delivered with a three-pointer that sealed the win for Cleveland. "This is what I came back for," James said afterward. "I'm home."

Kyrie Irving shoots the three-pointer that helped Cleveland get the win during Game 7 of the 2016 NBA Finals.

James holds trophies and celebrates the 2016 win with teammates.

FUN FACT

The 2016 NBA championship was the first time the Warriors had lost three games in a row in three years.

NEVER WALK ALONE

The Liverpool soccer team were **underdogs** in the 2005 Champions League final. They were playing against Milan, one of the best teams of the past 10 years. It didn't start off well for Liverpool. By halftime, Milan was up 3–0. The Milan players were all smiles, waving to their families in the stands and joking around.

When the players came out in the second half, Liverpool fans were singing "You'll Never Walk Alone." The song about togetherness likely inspired the team. Nine minutes into the half, midfielder Steven Gerrard scored on a **header**. The crowd started to get excited, and Liverpool added two more quick goals. The game stayed tied until extra time, when Liverpool won on a thrilling shoot-out.

The Liverpool team celebrates their thrilling 2005 victory on the field.

Afterward, Liverpool defender Djimi Traoré spoke about the Milan players' behavior in the first half. "You could tell that they thought it was game over," he said. "That just gave us even more motivation to come back."

CHAPTER 2
CRUSHING CURSES

Sports fans and players tend to be **superstitious**. Maybe you have a lucky shirt. Maybe you've worn a rally cap hoping it would help your team come back. One common superstition is how people sometimes try to explain bad luck. They often blame it on a curse.

BREAKING THE CURSE OF THE BILLY GOAT

The Chicago Cubs played in the 1945 World Series. At one game at Chicago's Wrigley Field, the owner of the Billy Goat Tavern, William Sianis, wanted to bring his pet goat into the stadium. But his smelly pet wasn't allowed in. The tavern owner angrily proclaimed, "You are going to lose this World Series, and you are never going to win another World Series again."

The Cubs invited Sam Sianis, nephew of William and the Billy Goat Tavern's owner, to come with his goat to a 1984 game.

For a long time, the Curse of the Billy Goat held true. The Cubs did lose the 1945 Series. The team didn't get to another World Series until 2016. Even then, the curse seemed to stick. The Cubs fell behind three games to one against Cleveland. But they fought back to tie it up.

Then in Game 7, the team blew a three-run lead. It seemed like the curse would hold again. But in the 10th inning, the Cubs miraculously scored two runs. They held on to finally get the curse-busting win!

The Cubs in a celebratory huddle

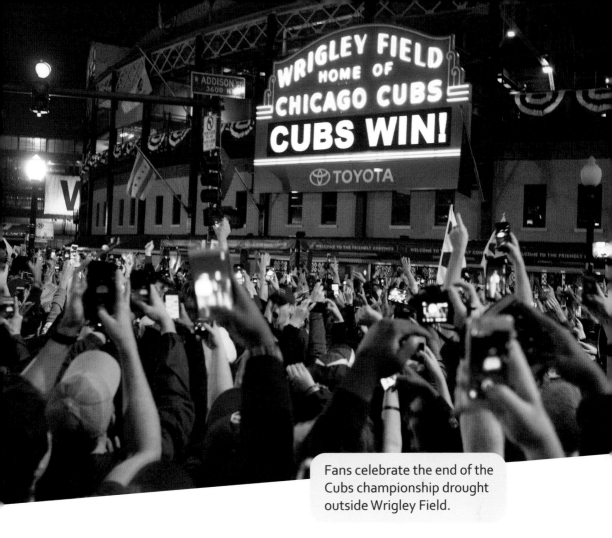

Fans celebrate the end of the Cubs championship drought outside Wrigley Field.

FUN FACT

Before 2016, the Cubs had not won a World Series since 1908. The 108-year-old championship title drought was the longest in professional sports history.

RED SOX REVERSE THE CURSE

Before becoming "the Bambino" and baseball's greatest slugger, Babe Ruth played for the Boston Red Sox. But in 1920, the Red Sox sold him to the **rival** New York Yankees. The Red Sox had won several World Series in the early 1900s. But after dealing away Ruth, they didn't win another title for 84 years. Meanwhile, the Yankees won 26 championships during that time. Fans said it was the Curse of the Bambino.

Babe Ruth

But things changed in 2004. The Red Sox faced the Yankees in the American League Championship Series (ALCS). They were down three games to none. In Game 4, they were losing in the ninth inning and faced one of history's greatest postseason relief pitchers: Mariano Rivera.

Ortiz smashes the game-winning home run during Game 4 of the 2004 ALCS.

But the Sox managed to get a walk, a daring stolen base, and a single to tie the game. That set the stage for David Ortiz, who crushed a **walk-off** homer in the 12th inning. The Red Sox never looked back. First, they completed the comeback to win the ALCS. Then they swept the St. Louis Cardinals in the World Series.

CHAPTER 3
CHALLENGES AND SUCCESS

Sometimes the toughest comeback isn't against an opponent. Some athletes have to overcome the cruel setbacks that life throws at them.

TOUGHER THAN A SHARK

Bethany Hamilton

Bethany Hamilton was just 8 years old when she decided she wanted to be a pro surfer. She worked hard to get there. But in 2003, when Bethany was 13, her dreams were put on hold in a big way. She was out surfing with her best friend's family when she was attacked by a 14-foot (4.3-meter) tiger shark. It took off her arm.

Hamilton was rushed back to shore and to the hospital. She lost about 60 percent of her blood, but she survived. However, that wasn't the end of her story. Amazingly, Bethany was back to surfing just 26 days after the attack. And she saw her dreams come true when she turned pro in 2007.

Hamilton competes in the World Surfing Games in California in 2006.

A NIGHTMARE AT CENTER COURT

Monica Seles was once the greatest tennis player in the world. She won seven Grand Slam tournaments from 1991 to 1993. She was ranked number one in the world for 91 weeks in a row. She was living a dream life. But on April 30, 1993, a **deranged** fan took it all away from her. He came onto the court during a match in Hamburg, Germany, and stabbed her in the back.

Incredibly, Seles recovered from the injury in a few weeks. Yet the emotional pain kept her away from tennis. It was too painful and scary for her to return to the court.

Sports Illustrated edition showing Seles after the April 1993 attack

Seles goes for the ball during the 1996 U.S. Open tournament.

Eventually Seles realized that tennis was what made her happy. She trained and came back. Her first tournament in almost two and a half years was the Canadian Open. She dominated it.

COMEBACK IN THE CUP SERIES

Kyle Busch had never won a NASCAR Cup Series Championship. But many believed 2015 would finally be his year. Then a brutal crash in February changed all that. Busch's legs were severely injured. Instead of winning it all, many wondered if he'd ever race, or walk, again.

Emergency workers attend to Busch after his #54 car (far left) hit the wall on February 21, 2015.

Busch holds up the Cup Series trophy in 2015.

Busch worked hard on his rehab and recovered more quickly than expected. Though few believed it was possible, he was back to racing that same season. He'd missed 11 races, so he had to make up a lot of points to qualify for the **playoffs**. He raced well. At one point he even won three races in a row. Busch completed his dramatic comeback by winning his first-ever Cup Series Championship.

CHAPTER 4

IT'S NEVER TOO LATE

Many great athletes find it hard to walk away from the game they love. Once they do leave, coming back at an older age can be especially challenging.

REPEAT THE THREE-PEAT

Michael Jordan wanted something different. After winning three straight championships with the Chicago Bulls, he retired from basketball to try pro baseball. In 1994, he joined a AA minor-league team of the Chicago White Sox. But he missed basketball. It was his real love. So in 1995 he released a two-word press release: "I'm back."

In 1995, Jordan decided to come back to the NBA.

Jordan goes for a layup in a game against the New York Knicks on March 28, 1995.

The next night, Jordan rejoined the Bulls in the middle of the season. He hadn't played in nearly two years. But he suited up against the Indiana Pacers and put up 19 points. As the season went on, he regained his old form. The Bulls finished 13–4 with Jordan on their team. They lost to Orlando in the semifinals.

Jordan didn't have the **stamina** to lift his team the way he used to. But he accepted the challenge. In the off-season, he trained hard to get back into shape. He and the Bulls then went on to win the next three NBA titles from 1996 to 1998.

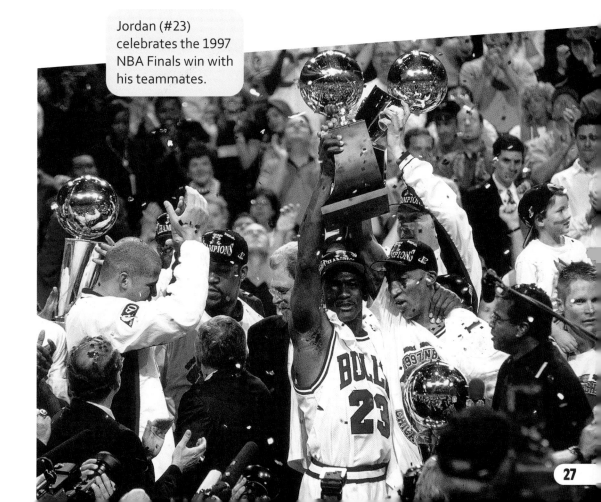

Jordan (#23) celebrates the 1997 NBA Finals win with his teammates.

THE RETURN OF BIG GEORGE

In the 1970s, George Foreman had been the heavyweight boxing champion of the world. When he retired in 1977, he became a Christian minister. "For 10 years, I didn't even make a fist," he said later. "I didn't train. I didn't box."

However, Foreman eventually ran out of money. The one way he knew to make money was by boxing. But he was overweight and out of shape. Foreman began to train. He dropped a lot of weight. Then in 1994 he challenged the current heavyweight boxing champ, Michael Moorer. Foreman knocked him out with a fierce right hook. He reclaimed the championship at age 45! It was more than 20 years after he'd first won it.

The referee raises Foreman's arm up in victory after he knocked out Michael Moorer on November 5, 1994.

FUN FACT

After earning enough money to last a while, Foreman retired again in 1997. He was the oldest boxer to ever hold the title of heavyweight champion.

GLOSSARY

deranged
(di-RAYNJD)
mentally unsound

header (HED-uhr) a shot
or pass a soccer player
makes with their head

momentum
(moh-MEN-tuhm)
energy gained by a series
of positive events

playoffs (PLAY-awfs)
a series of competitions
after the regular season to
determine a champion

rival (RYE-vuhl)
someone you play against
where there is a strong
feeling of competition

stamina
(STAM-uh-nuh)
the energy and strength
to keep doing something
for a long time

superstitious
(soo-pur-STI-shuhs)
having beliefs that
something can affect the
outcome of a future event

underdog
(UHN-der-dawg) the
team or player that is
considered more likely to
lose in a game

walk-off (WALK-off)
a score that ends a game

READ MORE

Doeden, Matt. *Coming Up Clutch: The Greatest Upsets, Comebacks, and Finishes in Sports History.* Minneapolis: Millbrook Press, 2018.

Lyon, Drew. *Pro Football's All-Time Greatest Comebacks.* North Mankato, MN: Capstone, 2019.

Marsico, Katie. *Surviving a Shark Attack: Bethany Hamilton.* Minneapolis: Lerner Publications, 2019.

INTERNET SITES

Ducksters: LeBron James
ducksters.com/sports/lebron_james.php

International Tennis Hall of Fame: Monica Seles
tennisfame.com/hall-of-famers/inductees/
monica-seles

Kiddle: Babe Ruth Facts for Kids
kids.kiddle.co/Babe_Ruth

INDEX

ABOUT THE AUTHOR

Eric Braun is the author of dozens of books for young readers. His favorite things to write about include history, fairy tales, and especially sports. One of his books was read by an astronaut on the International Space Station. Besides stories, he loves bike riding, camping, adventures, and wearing hats.

Learn more at heyericbraun.com.